THE HIMALAYAS

CHARLES W. MAYNARD

The Rosen Publishing Group's
PowerKids Press ™
New York

For Janice, who has climbed many mountains with me

Published in 2004 by The Rosen Publishing Group, Inc.
29 East 21st Street, New York, NY 10010

First Edition

Editor: Frances E. Ruffin

Book Design: Emily Muschinske

Photo Credits: Cover and p. 1 © Craig Lovell/CORBIS; pp. 4 (top), 8 (bottom), 20 © Imagebank/Getty Images, Inc., p. 4 (bottom) © Eric DePalo; p. 7 © GeoAtlas; p. 8 (top) courtesy of NASA/CORBIS; p. 8 (center) © Simon Fraser/Science Photo Library/Photo Researchers; pp. 11 (right), 15 (top) © Stone/Getty Images, Inc., p. 11 (left) © Maria Stenzel/National Geographic Image Collection; p.19 © National Geographic Image Collection; p. 12 © Geoff Bryant/Photo Researchers; p. 15 (bottom) © Tim Fitzharris/AG Pix; p. 16 © MacDuff Everton/The Image Works; p. 17 © Dani/Jeske/Earth Scenes; p. 20 (inset) © CORBIS.

Maynard, Charles W. (Charles William), 1955–
The Himalayas / Charles W. Maynard.
    v. cm.—(Great mountain ranges of the world)
Contents: Rooftop of the world—When continents collide—A land of contrasts—Abode of snow—Varied vegetation—Amazing animals—Many mountain cultures—On top of the world—The abominable snowman—Mapping and protecting the unknown.
  ISBN 0-8239-6694-1
1. Himalaya Mountains—Juvenile literature. [1. Himalaya Mountains.] I. Title.
  DS485.H6 M378 2004
  915.496—dc21

                                                                                    2002013503

Manufactured in the United States of America

CONTENTS

K2
28,250 feet
(8,611 m)

ANNAPURNA
26,504 feet
(8,078 m)

CHO OYU
26,750 feet
(8,153 m)

MANASLU
26,781 feet
(8,163 m)

MAKALU
27,824 feet
(8,481 m)

EVEREST
29,028 feet
(8,848 m)

LHOTSE
27,923 feet
(8,511 m)

KANCHEN-
JUNGA
28,169 feet
(8,586 m)

ROOFTOP OF THE WORLD

The Himalayan mountain range includes the highest peaks in the world. Fourteen of the peaks rise more than 26,247 feet (8,000 m) above **sea level**. The Himalayas stretch for 1,550 miles (2,494 km) in central Asia. From China's border, they travel through Burma, Nepal, Tibet, and Bhutan, dip south to India, and spread west, ending in Afghanistan. These mountains form the boundaries between many countries on the **continent** of Asia.

The highest peak in the Himalayas, and thus in the world, is Mount Everest at 29,028 feet (8,848 m). Mt. Everest, on the border of Nepal and China, is named for Sir George Everest of Great Britain. Everest (1790–1866) led the **survey** of India from 1830 to 1843.

The name "Himalaya" comes from Sanskrit words that mean **abode**, or house, of snow. Sanskrit is an ancient language that was spoken in India. Because the highest mountains on Earth are in the Himalayas, these amazing mountains are also called the Rooftop of the World.

The mountain peaks in this photo of the Tibetan plateau in China show why the Himalayas are called the Rooftop of the World. The people of Nepal call Mt. Everest "Sagarmatha," which means Mother of the Universe. The chart shows the Himalayas' tallest peaks.

When Continents Collide

The Himalayas are young compared to other mountain ranges in the world. The Himalayas began forming from 60 to 65 million years ago. The Appalachian range in the eastern United States is from 250 to 300 million years old.

The surface of Earth, called the crust, is made of huge slabs of rock called plates. These plates have moved slowly over millions of years, sometimes bumping into each other. When the plates bump together, the crust is pushed up and it forms mountains. Scientists call the movement of Earth's crust **plate tectonics**. About 50 million years ago, the Indian **subcontinent** began to bump into a land mass called Eurasia, which formed Europe and Asia. That event caused part of the Eurasian land mass to wrinkle, forming the Himalayas. These huge wrinkles are called fold mountains.

MOUNTAIN FACT

Even today, the tectonic plates are still moving, and the Himalayas are still growing. The Himalayas are getting taller by about 1 inch (2.5 cm) every five years.

The Himalayan mountains are part of the land in many countries, from China to Afghanistan.

RUSSIAN FEDERATION

KAZAKHSTAN

MONGOLIA

INNER MONGOLIA

KYRGYZSTAN

SINKIANG

TAJIKISTAN

8611
▲K2

Kunlun Shan

CHINA

AFGHANISTAN

KASHMIR

TIBET

Himalayas

8848
▲Mt Everest

NEPAL

PAKISTAN

INDIA

This picture of a huge, snakelike glacier in the Himalayas was taken from the space shuttle Atlantis.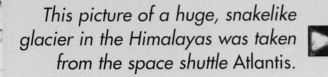

Over time, this glacier on the Tibet side of Mt. Everest has carved out the large valley shown in this photograph.

The Ganges River in India was formed by a glacier, high in the Himalayas. The Ganges is sacred for people of the Hindu religion.

Mountains Build Up and Wear Away

The peaks of the Himalayas were part of the ocean floor millions of years ago. Plate tectonic forces pushed the sea floors into high mountains. Some rocks near the highest peaks of the Himalayas are limestone. Limestone is a kind of rock that is made up of the **fossils** of sea creatures that lived and died millions of years ago.

As the Himalayas rise, other forces are working to wear them down. Over millions of years, gigantic **glaciers** slowly carve large valleys through the high mountains. As the snow and ice of the peaks melt, they form rivers. India's great Ganges River begins in the Himalayas.

India's and Nepal's great plains lie south of the range. The high Tibetan **plateau** lies to the north. In between, the Himalayas have three different **climate** zones. The highest snow-covered peaks lie in the Great Himalayas. The Lesser Himalayas have peaks between 6,000 and 15,000 feet (1,829–4,572 m) tall and are covered with forests and **fertile** valleys. The lowest, southernmost peaks are the Outer Himalayas. They are called foothills, and they have wide valleys and rivers.

A Land of Contrasts

Wide differences of **altitude** in the Himalayas create the many climates found there. The valleys of the Outer Himalayas, such as those in India and Burma, are **subtropical** with hot days and plenty of rain. The valleys of the Lesser Himalayas have a **temperate** climate. Average summer day **temperatures** there are from 60°F to 77°F (16°C–25°C). Winters are cooler. The Kathmandu valley of Nepal, in the temperate zone, is populated with many farms and several cities.

Most of the year's rainfall of 60 inches (152 cm) comes with **monsoon** winds from June through September. The eastern Himalayas receive more rain. The Himalayas affect the climate of central Asia by blocking cold weather from the north and humid weather from the south. The high Plateau of Tibet, to the north in China, is dry and dusty. The winters there are cold and long.

MOUNTAIN FACT

THE HIGHEST PEAKS IN THE GREAT HIMALAYAS ARE FROZEN WORLDS. SNOW AND ICE STAY ON THE GROUND YEAR-ROUND. EVEN THE VALLEYS ARE COLD AND DESERTLIKE, WITH NO TREES AND FEW PLANTS. ATOP MT. EVEREST THE OXYGEN IN THE AIR IS ONLY ONE-THIRD OF THAT AT SEA LEVEL. IT IS DIFFICULT FOR PLANTS, ANIMALS, AND HUMANS TO LIVE THERE.

Nepal's Kathmandu valley has several cities. The climate is mild enough for farming.

The snowcapped peak Annapurna is seen in the distance from this fertile valley in Nepal.

VARIED VEGETATION

The altitudes and climates in the Himalayas support many types of plant life. Rainfall, temperatures, and **oxygen** all affect the species of trees and plants that live in the mountains and in the valleys. The Outer Himalayas, once covered with a rich, tropical forest, have been **harvested**. The land is now either farmed or used to graze goats and other livestock. Pine, oak, and poplar trees grow in the Lesser Himalayas. People have cut down many of these trees, which has caused **erosion**. Tree roots are necessary for keeping soil in place on steep mountainsides. They keep the soil from washing away in rain or blowing away in high winds. Even though many of the steep slopes no longer have trees, beautiful wildflowers color the mountainsides. Orchids, lilies, anemones, poppies, and rhododendron flowers flourish among the mountains and valleys of the Lesser Himalayas. The tree line in the Great Himalayas is about 16,000 feet (4,877 m). Trees will not grow above this level because of the high altitude and the cold.

◄ *Blue poppies grow in the Himalayan woodlands.* Inset: *During summers goat herders, such as the man pictured here, move their livestock to graze high up on the Himalayan plains.*

Amazing Animals

Leopards, tigers, deer, and Indian rhinoceroses were once plentiful in the forests of the Outer Himalayas. When people cut down the trees for lumber, the forests changed and so did the types and numbers of animals that lived in them. Black bears, leopards and other cats, and the muntjac, a deer known for making a barking sound, now live in the few existing forests.

The Great Himalayas, a land of few people, are home to wolves, snow leopards, small, bushy-tailed marmots, and musk deer. A kind of tiny black spider lives as high as 22,500 feet (6,858 m).

The **yak** is a Tibetan ox that lives on high plateaus and in the mountains. It likes the cold, dry climate. People raise yaks to carry heavy loads and to pull carts. Yaks are a source of milk and meat. Yak hair is woven to make rope and cloth, and yak skin is used for leather.

MOUNTAIN FACT

THE WILD YAK IS A HUGE ANIMAL WITH LONG, BROWN-BLACK HAIR FORMING A THICK COAT. MALE YAKS CAN BE 6 ½ FEET (2 M) TALL AT THE SHOULDERS. THEY CAN WEIGH MORE THAN 2,000 POUNDS (907 KG).

A yak, shown here with a Tibetan family, is a common sight in the Himalayas.

A rare sight is the beautiful snow leopard, which is hunted for its fur.

The women shown here are picking tea leaves in West Bengal, India. West Bengal is at the warmer, southern end of the Himalayan mountain range.

MANY MOUNTAIN CULTURES

About 40 million people live in the Himalayas. The Himalayas pass through the Indian states. The Himalayas also lie in the kingdoms of Nepal and Bhutan, as well as in Tibet.

Many of the people who live in the southern countries of the Outer Himalayas and Lesser Himalayas are of Indian origin and practice the **Hindu** religion. North of India, most Tibetan people are **Buddhist**. Nepal has 35 separate **ethnic groups**.

Most people of the Himalayas are farmers who grow fruits and grains and who herd livestock. The **Sherpa** people live in Nepal's Great Himalayas. The Sherpas are tribespeople who came from Tibet and settled in the steep-sided valleys of the Himalayas. Sherpas are known as the best guides for climbers of these mountains.

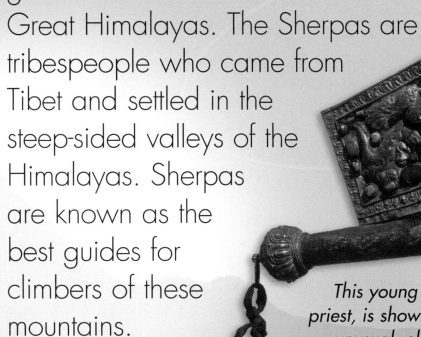

This young monk, or priest, is shown with an unusual, old trumpet that is played by monks in the Himalayas.

On Top of the World

The Himalayas were some of the last mountains on Earth to be explored. Ancient spice and silk trade routes between China and India wound through the high mountain passes between India and Tibet. A Spanish priest drew one of the first maps of the area in 1590. In 1852, British surveyors claimed that Peak XV was the highest peak in the world. It was later named Mt. Everest.

After several attempts, George Mallory and Andrew Irvine set out to climb Mt. Everest on June 8, 1924. They never returned. On May 29, 1953, Tenzing Norgay, a Sherpa, and Edmund Hillary, of New Zealand, became the first to reach Everest's peak. Since then, many climbers who have tried to scale this mountain have died from the freezing temperatures and the low oxygen. However, hundreds have reached Everest's peak, the top of the high Himalayas.

MOUNTAIN FACT: In 1999, an expedition searched for clues to the 1924 disappearance of George Mallory and Andrew Irvine. The team found George Mallory's body at more than 25,000 feet (7,620 m). After removing a few articles from his pockets, the team buried Mallory on the north face of Mt. Everest.

Left: *Mallory and Irvine are photographed at the beginning of their attempt to climb Everest.*
Right: *A woman climbs a frozen waterfall in the Khumbu range of the Himalayas.*

Mapping and Protecting the Himalayas

One early challenge to exploring the Himalayas was mapping its many high, snow-covered peaks. Today aircraft and **satellites** make exact maps possible. **Geologists**, **geographers**, and other scientists are still working to understand the Rooftop of the World better. Some areas of the Himalayas are being protected by several governments so that **endangered** plants and animals will be saved. The Sagarmatha National Park of Nepal is one example of this effort. The entire park is located above 9,700 feet (2,957 m). The government of Nepal set aside this special place to protect animals, plants, and mountain scenery. The Sherpa people are allowed to live in the national park. Although only a few people will ever climb the mountains, people come from all over the world to look with wonder at these mysterious high peaks and their steep valleys, large glaciers, and swift rivers. The Himalayas remain among Earth's most wonderful places.

In this computerized satellite view of the Himalayas, the snow appears to be blue, and the mountains green. Inset: Edmund Hillary (left) and Tenzing Norgay (right) were eating breakfast before setting out to climb Mt. Everest.

THE ABOMINABLE SNOWMAN

People who follow the Hindu and Buddhist religions in the Himalayas consider these mountains to be sacred. The Ganges, a sacred river to the Hindu people, begins from the snows of the Himalayas. The mountains were the "abode of the gods" to people who believed that the most powerful gods lived on the snowy peaks.

The Sherpas and Tibetans tell legends, or tales, about the yeti, who is also known as the Abominable Snowman. It is said that the name "yeti" comes from the Sherpa words *yah*, meaning rock, and *teh*, meaning animal. The yeti is believed to be a large, hairy creature that is bigger and stronger than a human.

There are no photographs or other proof to show that the yeti lives in the Himalayas. However, stories are told of yeti that attack and kill yaks in the high meadows. The religious beliefs and the stories about the yeti show that many people consider the Himalayas to be special mountains with many mysteries yet to be solved.

GLOSSARY

abode (uh-BOHD) A home.

altitude (AL-tih-tood) The height above Earth's surface.

Buddhist (BOO-dist) A person who practices the faith of Buddhism.

climate (KLY-mit) The kind of weather a certain area has.

continent (KON-tin-ent) One of the seven great masses of land on Earth.

endangered (en-DAYN-jerd) In danger of no longer existing.

erosion (ih-ROH-zhun) The wearing away of land over time.

ethnic groups (ETH-nik GROOPS) Groups of people that have the same race, culture, or language, or who belong to the same country.

fertile (FER-tul) Good for making and growing things.

fossils (FAH-sulz) The hardened remains of dead animals or plants.

geographers (jee-AH-gruh-ferz) Scientists who study the features of Earth.

geologists (jee-AH-luh-jists) Scientists who study the structure of Earth.

glaciers (GLAY-shurz) Large masses of ice that move down a mountain or along a valley.

harvested (HAR-vist-ed) Having gathered a season's crops.

Hindu (HIN-doo) Someone who believes in the Hindu religion of India.

monsoon (mon-SOON) Strong winds in the Indian Ocean and southern Asia.

oxygen (OK-sih-jen) A gas that has no color, taste, or odor, and is necessary for people and animals to breathe.

plateau (pla-TOH) A broad, flat, high piece of land.

plate tectonics (PLAYT tek-TAH-niks) The study of the moving pieces of Earth's crust.

satellites (SA-til-yts) Machines in space that circle Earth and are used to track weather.

sea level (SEE LEH-vul) The height of the top of the ocean.

Sherpa (SHERP-ah) A person from Tibet who lives in the Nepal region of the Himalayas.

subcontinent (sub-KON-tin-ent) A land mass that is part of one of Earth's seven great land masses.

subtropical (sub-TRAH-pih-kul) Just outside the warmest parts of Earth.

survey (ser-VAY) To measure land.

temperate (TEM-puh-rit) Not too hot or too cold.

temperatures (TEM-pruh-cherz) How hot or cold something is.

yak (YAK) A large type of ox found in Central Asia.

Index

Web Sites

Due to the changing nature of Internet links, PowerKids Press has developed an online list of Web sites related to the subject of this book. This site is updated regularly. Please use this link to access the list:

www.powerkidslinks.com/gmrw/himalaya/